So Many Mouths at the End of All Beauty

Alex M. Frankel

Deep Sett Press
Tucson, Arizona
2023

ISBN - 978-1-940830-38-4
LOC - 2022952181

Cover design by Robin Wyatt Dunn

By Alex M. Frankel

My Father's Lady, Wearing Black

Birth Mother Mercy

*A Decade of Sundays: L.A.'s Second Sunday Poetry Series,
The First Ten Years: 2009-2019*

Flame at Door and Raisin and Other Stories

In Memory of
Tonya Levy Lemberg
(1961-2022)

*In the womb of every soul sits a cripple
without an axiom to his name.*

—Charles Aerdnaissor

Table of Contents

But If There Is No God,
  Then We Pray to Oriana Grand? 3

People Who Are Asleep or in Love Do Not Know
  Whether a Child With a Match Is Watching 5

Testimony From the Horrendous Sinkhole
  Outside Tom's Restaurant 7

The Ecstasies of Sir Knut 7-Around 9

Sermon of the Silentiary 11

Rounds of Tiredness 13

Profession of Faith of the YouTube Commenter 15

Incomprehensions of Sleep 17

Fuck Me All You Want but No Feelings 18

In a Heart of Alleys, Trash Cans Burn Sublime 20

The Aging Priest and Bieber Nut 21

Without Her, We Could by No Means Be 22

McLeod, Schmegelsky & Sons 23

Dirty Heads and a Smell of Slime 25

Banana Statues With Feet
 and Carpe-Diem Teeth 26

After a Meeting of Fame-Seekers Anonymous 28

Corpses at Evening 30

I Try for Love Again, It's 1991 in the 909 32

Old Hiram Splitpenny 33

A Sri Lankan Truthsayer 35

But If There Is No God, Then We Pray to Oriana Grand?

Alexander de Grote perished from a lack of Twitter fans
on the nineteen-thousandth night of his beauty.

Like most of us he lived for all kinds of likes
in the flamelight of his machines.
Alex was a diamond worker
in the very mouth of Rome.

He died at the feet of Invictissimus King H—
or a statue of Such in the town center.
A sect of astrologers spotted the corpse,
got a load of students to help.
"It's a shame," they said,
"but who the hell was he?"

A sullen crowd attended
in front of the College of Prosperity.
Ten men-to-be-ordained, passing by,
beheld an image they called "true sunshine at night"
and took it as a sign for this old stumble world.

The sirens bloated, the polyglot crowd thinned out.
They clearly didn't give a Bronx dollar.
A dog of some sort came to sit on the corpse
and, crying, formed a miniature oasis of respect.
Some said it knew the corpse.
Some said it was just crying for the sirens.

A few translations claim this story ended there.
Most others say that two blocks north
a parade of Oriana Grand fanatics
happened to come marching in boisterous tribute.
It was fifty-two million souls strong,
including heads of industry
and many other members of the Game.
No amount of soldiery could contain such a horde.
God was only Prime Minister
for the first eighty-five seconds of this Earth,
but Oriana: in kimono and heels, she sat in a sedan chair
held aloft by girls and men and the axis of life,
a moment nineteen thousand years in the making.
People held phones and chanted for Oriana
and it was beautiful for a long time.

People Who Are Asleep or in Love Do Not Know Whether a Child With a Match Is Watching

I caught a little bird and glued it to a rock
and painted the bird and rock
the color of my hand-painted house.
I started and knew I would never stop.
My windshield is splattered with eyelids.
If my wind moves north, my rock moves west.
They call me a compassionless hoodlum
because I can't let go of the game.
My shoes are wooden boxes or purple carrots.
Automobiles groan when I pass by.
When I bump into a fig tree in the air
it'll run alongside me for hours begging pardon.
I'm made of bone power, this is development hell,
no one can play my music.

On the school bus I'm busy getting pregnant.
School is too small for small boys like me.
Crime is anger that can't go to sleep.
There was an old man and he was upset
by the light from his husband's light in their room
so I inserted my knife into both of them.
Now both men carry their love's light clean
into the great light of the Throne Room.
I wear the skirt I was born with.

When I wake up, Mommy says I go a-trumpeting,
she says I follow a puppy god.
I wake up but my mouse gut is well asleep.
Time for SFUSD.
The principal has proclaimed this Despair Week.
Once at a Giants game I yanked Mayor Alioto's hand
and asked him to ask me how I loved my Giannini school.
It's hell I said and the riots began.

**Testimony From the Horrendous Sinkhole
Outside Tom's Restaurant**

My favorite former friend
sits by his fire in long johns
decades after he returned my calls.
The lauded philosopher is going bald!
Syllogisms fall from his neck and flee.
He believes there's no breath but what he breathes.
Four naps in five hours.
His books won't live.

A sinkhole twelve floors below
has filled with hundreds of failed philosophers
anxious for my former friend to fall.
Some of them snooze to Prosperity TV.
Many are hunting Upper West Side rats
hoping for at least one meal in their systems.
Someone remarks it's like existing in Belarus.

My former friend, named Fred Kitchener,
knowing the philosophers are hungry below
(but not to save him in a life net)
twitches into his fifth nap of the night:
He's floating in a bed of land
surrounded by night houses of the sane.
He stalks through a palace of half-crafted rooms
and, in the shabbiest of royal kitchens,
finds me on my knees scouring the floor:
"Fifty years, four months, nine days
when you could so effortlessly, as a gesture,

have picked up the phone to inquire about me
or my old dad, always so fond of you."
"Oh Alex!" But Kitchener is falling now
and in the pit we're on him, we strip him,
the gospel says love your enemies but no can do.
I grab his Swiss army knife and his Mastercard,
my counselor said "Let him go, get *present*"
but with fifty other good-for-nothings
here I am in the muck fighting over Fred's Rolex.

The Ecstasies of Sir Knut 7-Around

His wealth rises on scum everlasting.
He sees through the mind of a mathematical star
and so everywhere grow lady trees.
He's batty raising seven daughters
and adorning his wife Morbida Susy.
His face of uncurated skin with a mouth at its center
has no other features but half an eyelid.
The face of a rejected shoulder.
When he steps to the right of his cypress
countless human teeth blow hectic in the wind
and bite into many a passer-by.
There's something sepulchral about his happiness.
With a half eyelid, he holds underlings suspended
so that a building's windows can't stop discussing.
His sweat flows upward in a hundred arrows.
With one frown, he can destroy stocks or crops,
but only after a blistering night's rest.
I love his face when it falls, and his one lid,
unlike the lid of anyone else
when it attempts to shut and get sleep
and then succeeds in "soul"-enhancing slumber.
Like me, he's a skull's son,
like me, he throws ultraviolet depressions
so that the outer circle of his world wraps wounded
yet the idea of a priest makes him shudder-scared.
Unlike me, he's not getting old.
"Abyss yourself," he chuckles every time envy wins
and I try to slay his meager body dead.
I'll always be a backseat assistant,

his bald pate will always celebrate riches.
At night I'm in charge of his withered arms.
I soak them in painful towels.
If he scowls, it rains pesticides, but if he laughs
it's like jasmine outside his bay window
waiting for daylight's approval.

Sermon of the Silentiary

My clothes walked down to the beach
looking to toss and maybe to flutter,
my clothes made of alabaster and pearls
and faithless foundations
went down to the beach and shivered.
Dwarves marched near them bratty and weak.

The ocean's water foamed restfully.
Everyone avoided my unruly clothes
that held a glass of syrup to the light.
"Hey look it's dolphins out there" said a dwarf.
"Those are pirates dumbass" said his friend.
"This'll be our first hurricane" observed a third.
All sang the urine song.

Nuns came to batter the dwarves,
a real-life calamity
because the nuns had the eyes of stepmothers.
My clothes undressed themselves
there in front of the nuns and the dwarves
and the KFC that overlooked and oversaw everything.
Alabaster garments flew in the breeze
and so did sapphire socks and a miracle beanie
until the single glass of syrup hung suspended.

Nuns shooed every soul away and fled.
In the KFC authorities dialed urgent care.
No hint of my clothes in the first wind.
A thousand storks washed up lifeless
but just one pair of eyebrows saw fit to rise
as if in sprightly comment.

Rounds of Tiredness

To ask a Sunday if it will ever return…
it cannot or will not say it won't.
To ask a Chinese elm outside these ruins,
why we were thrown into such a futility of lore…
it shrugs, as if in deference to lightning.
To ask Dionysus the Unbelievable
what he does about the irksome dancers and athletes
who have wounded many of our dead
with a thousand lessons and a hundred precepts…
he just leers mischievously.

To pay a silver visit to Txhua Bloin
who died for life after a deadly race,
her fractures and teeth forgotten.
Within an assault of road lights
her water-raft drips and drops,
almost no poppies grow inside it.
To note her whips and beauty fingers,
how all day she gives birth and plays the balalaika.
To ask her to please open her book
and finally say how and why we woke up here
skinny, burned, stupid, shunned.
She births seven skeleton-babes, declares:
I know for a fact everyone's first days will sadden
but beyond that I cannot claim to know.
I'd ask the opinion of the stars
but they're a bunch of fraudsters,
they're time without a head, space without a hand.

I sense skepticism all round, I too was skeptical,
but Tuesday will roll by as surely as
it follows Monday, and like clockwork
unremember itself unfairly.
Welcome to a brutalist cloister devoid of clarity!

Her wig collapses,
her offspring drift away, a chorus of hot air balloons.
To try to shake her hand would be folly
for she only offers a sliver of a horse's hand,
baleful and porous.

Profession of Faith of the YouTube Commenter

Often poisonous waters from above pour into an ocean, and two tsunamis converge; I walk the ground between them. I am an ordinary woman with dreams of drowning, sometimes dreams of bodies of water, a creek, and suddenly there is water spreading like tsunami waves. One time I dreamed of Indonesia. Perhaps that was years ago. I ask God or Jesus who really am I and do I have a power of Seeing? Maybe this is the year I see Mama Mary, but I don't know. I remember my premonitions, even Japan, the spillage of 2011. Is there a second coming? I am a Catholic but sometimes I question about Jesus being Lord. I have a lot of love for myself in the world. If you want to join me, I might tell you something of the future. When I go to bed, I don't know what I am talking about, but I don't know. When I fought my father, I became overwhelmed by an obsessed person who ignored Jesus Christ. I know you don't know what I mean. I am wrong. I could not go anywhere to learn from the famous nations. I am a Catholic but do not believe in the end of the world. I always spin in the tsunami when the tsunami arrives. I don't like your parents or mine, and I don't like their soothsaying. I have never been to any place and have been schooled in no principles. I am so very happy to hear that I don't know how much I have learned. At the end of the way, I do not believe in the end. At one point, I was afraid and my heart exclaimed, "I am doing wrong, I want happiness forever!" If you want to join me, I might tell you about the future. I have never found the author of my book. At the end of the world, I will not think the end of the world has come. I wonder about the very young mother of Jesus. When I'm in a fight, I worry about who Jesus really is. And those who believe Allah, are they wrong? I do not understand God, but I want the world to live forever on the other side. Poison water strikes water, and tsunamis hit tsunami waves; I walk between them with dreams of drowning. I know what's going on with the world. I don't know who I am, but I have the strength of the day that my fathers had. I could reach 2025 alive. If you can join me, we might make sense of the future. It is possible to say more, but I am afraid for my heart. Have you ever found the author of your book? When the waters of the sea tumble into the sea, I will say the blind can satisfy the wishes of the blind. Jesus Christ based himself on me. I started to learn about Baba Vanga and the kind prophets. I am dreaming of a voice singing male and female. I want to go back, as the righteous masses go back in Exodus. In you I see a sad face you do not understand, but you need to write my good book. And if it is written in English, it cannot perish. Do not go anywhere to be taught by the prominent men. Seawater pours into seawater; I walk the ground above it. The sun wants to believe in me. If this is English, spears will not strike. I am the strength of the day.

Incomprehensions of Sleep

The sound of the house the wolf ate
seemed a violation of the soul's very protein
and promised a swift seaquake.

We entered the white mouth
of the burning monastery
and viewed, in a darkness surrounded by
land, dollars and branches,
the excitement of the original painting:

It was as if the snow had been tasked
with lying in rigid adherence to the shore
and the melting sea waves.
Stiff priestmonks kicked back and smoked.
Only the shadows of Ukrainian kids—
icons in every sense—ate ice cream.
Then the whole scene slid downstairs into
a glass of black pepper and ocean
and a treasury of boyfriend videos.
The weather worsened and disapproved.

Little did we know, as we exited the mouth,
how much had been stolen from us.
Wolves everywhere stabbed each other in the scalp.
Neither Ukraine nor Ohio functioned.
Little did we know, walking down aisles
and aisles of DuckDuckGo, that our faces, splitting
into three here or two there,
had quarreled themselves into
brittle walls of tenderloin for the pack.

Fuck Me All You Want but No Feelings

He felt the kiss-assault of his four voices:
Isabella the curvaceous Irishman
Gladys the CIA emergency rat
a dumb mutawakazi also known as God
and, finally, outranking all the above,
Disney Man the Human Purifier.
Clinging to sunscreen and anal freeze
and his father's eight-inch semi-automatic,
his eyes filled slowly with massage parlor, schoolyard,
church, Wal-Mart, Super Bowl, Supreme Court, U.N.
and other countries of lame chickens.
Isabella said "When you have a difficult eye in your life
there are many others who will see forever after
what your eyes look like" and Gladys said
"Blame the sea waves with their carousels and games"
and God said "When there's no love, there's love"
but Disney Man the Human Purifier thundered
"The brain of Bryce Canyon commands you: Kill."
He longed for deafness or sleep of night
but the choir of rascals didn't stop,
in fact they filled ballrooms with every wrong.
On Dad's Day he felt like a jock stud and loved it.
Enraged with a bangwank kiss, his twinky fingers worked,
unloaded every time he saw signs of socialism
or a mask or a black or brown face or an obscure word,
he sent forty-eight to eternal life, his four voices cheered
but Disney Man cheered the most uproarious.
A family of white birds flew up.
Then he lifted a burning football from its display case

and, with wise arrogance, drank its molten gold.
Ballet shoes and lacrosse sticks littered his gullet
happiness to happiness.

In a Heart of Alleys, Trash Cans Burn Sublime

I existed in just an inch of hotel
with a three-bedroom baby in a one-finger room.
It was the Alps of Aleppo Hotel in the Quarter.
I missed my mom and dressed as a good mom.
Lobby dogs lapped up the goop of sleepers liquefied.
The concierge spoke a language thought to have died out,
he sported a long white severity
adorned with Masonic shapes bad for the eyesight.
I lived on Tylenol and Excedrin.

I saw a woman in the feet of the wall
step by step she walked up the wall,
her wings had wings and she opened her beak—
"C'mon, Mary Pope, your boy's gotten sick of this,
let's not wake up the whole establishment."
When a storm escaped from her beak
a brute named Hot Clint wrested my baby away.

People talk and die, years pass, CNN in the background.
They say taxis ride to the hills and back
heavy with children from hotel bowels.
The taxis pass by the Alps of Aleppo
where hallways narrow and widen, clinging to a center.
They say my child at seventeen still wears baby things.
Tourist couples order kids from an app.
Under streetlamps of sleep I see my child,
harrowed by birth in his bassinet.

They say the two-headed boy who fathered my boy
still hovers in his lordly pebble by my gravesite.

The Aging Priest and Bieber Nut

Lean Bieber dropped from a tree, so I worshiped him
and fed him burritos, he burped and bit me,
I gave him my wages and gave him a Barbie.
After years he got to be grand and querulous
as if ruling over a saloon from very old times.
Shirtless, he slapped my cheek with his foot:
"This priest thing, wasn't it just to please your mom?
Am I right, Father Martin? Some believer!"
I finally stood up to him but hundreds laughed,
they called the FBI who shot my brain out
meaning now I live as if in molasses.
Bieber has aged, 25!, and smells like cigar smoke
while I wait in molasses for a new head.
How he romps, wears out his offspring and fans
and wears them around his waist,
conducts chainsaws that sail through the sky sawing.
My time is heavy, I'm sinking south of the game.
Near me a bishop writhes like a roach in a glue trap,
they say he's Bieber's victim, too.
Near me an archbishop moans, likewise a victim.
We sink south of the game on mouse wings.

Without Her, We Could by No Means Be

All night she gave birth to her husband
who came out shivering like a mule.
Just by being, he proved the worst of his kind
and yet, at first, she heaped on him her everything
as wings fell from wind chimes that guarded the wind.
His body's mind seemed the color of her body.
His head's eyes told tales of the Great War
packed with poor hygiene and lack of sleep.
"Stop overthinking things, hon" he told her.
"Stop throwing your defunct feet at me" she told him.
He claimed his vintage helmet held her right apostles
but the thumb-sized holy men waved hot iron rods
too close to her nipples and she cried.
Lightning unleashed sea-flies into the decrepit room.
"I'll name you Ephraim" she said
"because you've destroyed all hope."
All night she strangled her husband.
Over a rainbow, a phalanx of storks carried off his remains
but they froze into marble and slammed to earth.
Doctors and congressmen tended to the slabs
and tossed them back skyward.
Some as marble and some as storks and some as human parts
they flocked to the woman and pecked at her face
until she birthed a husband.
She knew to melt his extremities but not in time.
He slew her with a diamond brooch.

McLeod, Schmegelsky & Sons

We drove a 1936 Toyota Corolla
we were young and engine-crazed
and had plenty of lice and acne
but we were like tiger sharks too
in spite of our outdated machine.
We were flames in the face
of a decrepit male-frame tottering along
and ran him over solid good.
We saw a flashy queen-mother singing
an upbeat taco ditty to her kid,
we ran them over light and windy
but caught their undergarments in our nostrils.
Compassion flashed but didn't last.
The home invasion part was the funnest.
We nailed an old gold digger
to the antlers of her wall moose
and hung around eating marzipan
three nights before she croaked.
How fast was our hate? Couldn't say.
We were young on the journey of our minds
without arrow or trench coat or brick.
Then we fell into our radio.
We were drops of fleas dripping
from a frightened wildwest tree.

Now we bounce black and blue in the Furnace,
sunlights of darkness and commotion.
We're not us and hate it.
What happened to our eagles?

We're not able to understand
and want to understand what happens
when fathers fall, all things defiled.
This song will not calm down.
Our noses—noses of the once-great—
are stapled to each other for always.
Everything is loud and crying.
Are you by any chance crying for us?

Dirty Heads and a Smell of Slime

Three studs in the bunks below me
having mellifluous wet dreams
put me in mind of "Acropolis Face" Yuzhnaya Shree,
his muscular, apricot-scented body
and his words "If only I had more sex, I'd be gorgeous."
Like him I was admitted to the world in the 20th century,
have lived an unsolvable life with pigs, crops,
conservative beliefs, stupid fables
and pines whistling outside the tabernacle.
Three conscripts in the bunks below me
moan out some mumbo-jumbo and exhale
and I think of Romano Starwitt in his garments,
how there was nothing until he kissed my lips.
The asphalt in his tongue discovered smelly me!
He thought like an eggplant from the northern reaches
and morphed into a rank of organ pipes.
On the third road from the olive tree, tanks are raging.
In nine weeks all three studs will drop into boxes.
Sergeant Donut used to say "See, war is about
the breaking of ashtrays and the faint hedgehog smell
of two worlds in mourning. Peace,
on the other hand, is the dread of broken ashtrays."
Let juice swill for an hour, lads,
let it float upwards in butterfly cycles.
Let three soccer stars snore again,
electric dolls and grapefruits rotting in their cellars.
I sink with them into row houses and parks
and tar-kisses of the resurrection.

Banana Statues With Feet and Carpe-Diem Teeth

Waking up in Malibu, 2199 A.D.

My wake-up guide was a she
Kathleen Progress by name
webwasher and student of the nephron.
She had an f-colored elbow face
kindergarten legs and a doctornurse vibe.
Wheeling me into town
she fed me Tucson shrimp.
MySpace Shows every hour on the hour.
Throngs of beggar kids with Blackberries.
Insatiable graffiti and half-devoured possums.
On every door a portrait of Ivanka XIII.

Kathleen and her boss Glip Glandia
debriefed me for upwards of 200 hours.
Glip said: "We'll gift you a U21 soccer squad
sturdy, slutty and ready for use.
Just don't break them please.
And don't forget to thank the Empress
on World Altar 61 promptly at six tonight."
They handed me my Sincerity Key.

The surface of the earth, as you may have guessed,
was made of human bones and bird parts.
No one saw the sky because no one looked.
With my unfamous face and penguin way
I easily found the house, homey as a pool hall.
Skagtaard, the U21 captain, lay reading his *Jakarta Post*.

"You are corrupted," he said without looking up.
"Dependent on the alphas who envelope you.
I'm programmed into you, you have no depth.
braindead slut, you can't resist me."

Skagtaard reached out but with my Sincerity Key
I opened all of him up quick:
inside he was just wiring and goo.

My house held eleven statues of Ivanka
wounded 400 times in the last coup.
A chopper dropped leaflets down my chute.
I had eleven baby typewriters with T-Rex engines
but my hands and feet could no longer resolve.

Skagtaard managed thirteen last words:
"I will kiss your mind with MySpace buttons, please,
if you console my garden with Friendster hooch…"

After a Meeting of Fame-Seekers Anonymous

Moritz Inchlinger, fame-seeker,
slept bright for nearly five hundred years
on the doorstep of the orphanage.

The smell of orphans soothed him
ninety-nine million times a year.
He slept through wars and the lives of vipers.
He began to attract viewers, first two
then thirty-two, then three hundred thousand,
even actress Trish Keating paid attention
and Prime Minister Radcliffe took note.
Inchlinger persisted in the citadel of sleep.
On a bridge over his eyes appeared the Wizard Scout
who proclaimed "A likeness carved in ivory!"
The deaf heard the power of the thin fame-seeker
who slept in blue and white and blue sleep milk.
Generations of actors and scouts and prime ministers
watched over Inchlinger who did not speak or say.
The galaxy couldn't rest without checking in on him.
In sleep he learned the many lessons he didn't learn
but witnessed the mountain toast the moon.
So many mouths at the end of all beauty, in other words:
Inchlinger heard the tumult of the New One
and beheld the lightning of the Voice.

He was found in a pond on a Monday,
his body made strong by the pond.
Because the weather was clear and the weather was off

and the weather was clear
Cal Murphy, founder of Fame-Seekers Anonymous
and known to members as Friend Zero,
stopped by to respect the shy face and frame.
They say the corpse got five views, tops.

Corpses at Evening

Bodybuilders smelled the deadest.
Remembering a passion for summer and snorkeling
their eyes awoke to be stabbed with syringes.
Our governor, finding a goat on his couch,
opened the earth with a sword
revealing a slew of greasers bent
on conquest of our deathcare system.

At the request of Pharaoh, the Duke of Bavaria
had his sea lions robed and sat them on the Port Authority.
At the request of Pharaoh, the Duke of Bavaria
crowned himself Lord Protector of our Tri-State.
Corpses erupted everywhere: six-day-old corpses,
fourteen-day-old corpses, dilf and milf corpses
liberal and conservative corpses making popping sounds
because they remembered summer
and still craved facelifts and corrections.

Albino roaches feast on art nouveau tattoos.
High-schooler and collegian corpses are the sorriest.
The body's natural air-conditioning is broken,
they say a star above has it in for us.

Enter Errol Iguana—minor now major prophet—
pointing at Pharaoh's men in pineapple hats:
"Your beds shall be filled with stones
you shall cry out for your mothers as flies rise
from swamps, hunt you in their millions."

Exit Errol Iguana: He endured five days
of oriental death and three of regular death.
There are corpses made of sleep
but you'll find him stored in his icebox
among corpses made of waiting.

I Try for Love Again, It's 1991 in the 909

I am eighty-one he is eighteen cusses in his sleep
has a Wolverine inked across his face
I'm so crazy about his inkwork and biceps
that the first thought each morning is
He belongs to the universe not to me
it won't be long before he's reabsorbed
he'll only see me twice a week so life with Truong
is life without Truong I sleep in a wood and iron requiem
there he rocks on a rocking chair inside his mother
slurping juice in promiscuous soccer gear
he has a low-income way of standing at urinals
or snapping "Not in my mouth dood."
Sometimes he'll pop up barefoot out of the dark
with pizza and Corona Light and sing Beach Boys tunes
in a style he calls "midnight"
I hire a Riverside private eye to tail him
I have enough money to know the truth
because I need my wolverine
there is no me in me
even when he opens his shoes and legs
and agrees to stay the night and we wake up
giddy like we're both eleven
Truong and I spend hours planning his new tattoo
in the Norwegian mountains of my head
or by the waves of an unnatural sea
Truong offers me Vietnamese tea Truong cries out "Holy shit
they're like maggots!" takes a spatula once and for all
squishes the embryos out of my hair.

Old Hiram Splitpenny

Hiram's four Twitter followers
hoped to bury their little pal
in a famous king's whitewashed belfry.
In Hiram's honor they turned artificial stones
into edelweiss gems.
It was a time of human endarkenment
when cathedrals didn't know their stars.

The followers looked down at his plaintive jowls.
He had foreign-language fingers
and feathers where his toes should've been.
The followers saw better now than in life
how his father's wall had felled him,
Hiram Splitpenny, dime-store clerk and poet
who wrote about our inner cylinders,
the Sea of Pizarro with its waters
that subvert schools and chapels,
that even subvert miners of the region and his great aunt,
the would-be diva Tadapilia,
torn apart by critics at Lima's Covet Garden.

Royal cops rushed in. "Hiram *who*?
Let the birds feast on him."

So they washed him with breakfast
and many other ceremonies.
They watched birds and dogs feed
on Hiram's piteous cadaver.
They stood in hats and careless shoes
and said what's been said so often about anything
and talked until their follicles ached.
It was funny to hear anyone talk so long
about old Hiram Splitpenny.

A Sri Lankan Truthsayer

We heard the cries of the law courts
as they sank into molasses.
We heard teens sing "Sumer Is Icumin In"
to Muslims locked in wicker men.
And the smoke of the dark burned.
And from the disneymost compartments
of his sleep our Leader moaned
not for Pottersville but Berchtesgaden.
Even the simple among us heard whisperings
of *Bring back Robespierre, philosopher!*
If America fought Mexico, cables showed,
Mexico would win hands down, in other words:
a hundred jurists sworn to secrecy,
two hundred FBI handsomes
and the Under Secretary of State for Enlightenment
all led us to confirm the obvious:
lamps were going out across the plains.

And so that troubled January of 2020
some of us sought out a seer
Charles Aerdnaissor
a.k.a. the Blind Sleeping Boy of Sri Lanka
a convulsionary who awakens once a year
to hold court behind the curtains
of his four-poster bed.

As disciples took notes
Aerdnaissor grunted and squealed.
His apothegm-loaded voice called out
to our desperate delegation:

—"Why, sirs, your Jehovah is an amateur
easily cowed by influencers
inside the mercantile exchange."

—"Every book is a dream invented by wildfire
but the horse of wisdom is water."

—"What happens to the sun's arrowheads?
They live short lives that burn in your flashlight."

—"In the womb of every soul sits a cripple
without an axiom to his name."

—"Whence come the kendo swords of contentment?
Why, sirs, from incense and aloe vera."

—"Time can be extended or intended.
Contemplate the snows and icebergs of Sierra Leone."

—"Life is the story of worry.
Pain soup is the center of the early rainbow."

—"I am the son of puzzles.
I am the parent of puzzles.
In my quiver I house silver bugs
who'll give their livers for me."

—"Bumboclaat!
Why do well-fed, unhappy folks flock to this shrine?
Weaklings, all of you!"

Curtains parted
the "boy" poked out his head
(he was over a hundred with a wrestler physique).
Barking twice, he blessed us with an index finger.
"Open your noses and say tomorrow!"

Three organ chords shook the land
and Aerdnaissor died.
On rain ships they carried him into the monsoon.

His acolytes assured us
he'd only returned to his sleep state
but left these handwritten words:

After the Rage
(and the Rage will come)
flags will congeal, fizzle
into sculpture and sand.
Embers of Crusader gear
will grace the austral ponds.
Waves will die down
and a day will come for the lucky
to start over in caves.
Folks, it's Year One!
Your fossilized masters
still helpless in molasses
will become the funniest circus acts.

In front of an ancient mirror
a last glass Robespierre
will turn and turn on his music box
like a beloved husband.

Acknowledgments

Marriage (Lifespan Vol. 6) by Pure Slush: "Without Her, We Could by No Means Be" (Summer 2022)

Ouch! Collective: "The Aging Priest and Bieber Nut" and "Dirty Heads and a Smell of Slime" (2022)

The Museum of Americana: "I Try for Love Again, It's 1991 in the 909" (Fall 2022)

The Waiting Room by Nervous Ghost Press: "McLeod, Schmegelsky & Sons" (2023)

Otoliths: "The Ecstasies of Sir Knut 7-Around"; "Sermon of the Silentiary"; and "Rounds of Tiredness" (Summer 2022)

The Los Angeles Review of Los Angeles: "In a Heart of Alleys, Trash Cans Burn Sublime";
"Fuck Me All You Want but No Feelings"; and
"Incomprehensions of Sleep" (No. 17, July 2022)

Quantum Entanglement: "Old Hiram Splitpenny" (2023)

www.AlejoRoviraGoldner.com: "But If There Is No God, Then We Pray to Oriana Grand?";
"People Who Are Asleep or in Love Do Not Know Whether a Child With a Match Is Watching";
and "Profession of Faith of the YouTube Commenter" (2022)

www.SecondSundayPoetry.com: "After a Meeting of Fame-Seekers Anonymous" and "Corpses at Evening" (2021)

About the Author

Alex M. Frankel—who also occasionally publishes under the name Alejo Rovira Goldner—left Spain in 1995 to make a new life in Southern California. He has written poetry, plays, criticism, fiction and a fictionalized memoir. For many years he published reviews in *The Antioch Review* and also helped edit the journal as an assistant poetry editor. He has published in many quarterlies and has been nominated for a Best of the Net Prize as well as a Pushcart Prize. Lummox Press published his *Birth Mother Mercy* in 2013. His short story collection came out in 2022 and is entitled *Flame at Door and Raisin.*

He hosts the Second Sunday Poetry Series and his website is www.alexmfrankel.com.

Made in the USA
Columbia, SC
29 March 2024